Reiki Healing for Beginners

Improve Your Health, Increase Your Energy and Raise Your Vibration

© **Copyright 2018 - All rights reserved.**

This document is geared towards providing exact and reliable information regarding the topic and issue covered. The publication is sold with the idea that the publisher is not required to render an accounting, officially permitted, or otherwise, qualified services. If advice is necessary, legal or professional, a practiced individual in the profession should be ordered.

- From a Declaration of Principles which was accepted and approved equally by a Committee of the American Bar Association and a Committee of Publishers and Associations.

In no way is it legal to reproduce, duplicate, or transmit any part of this document in either electronic means or in printed format. Recording of this publication is strictly prohibited and any storage of this document is not allowed unless with written permission from the publisher. All rights reserved.

The information provided herein is stated to be truthful and consistent, in that any liability, in terms of inattention or otherwise, by any usage or abuse of any policies, processes, or directions contained within is the solitary and utter responsibility of the recipient reader. Under no circumstances will any legal responsibility or blame be held against the publisher for any reparation, damages, or monetary loss due to the information herein, either directly or indirectly.

Respective authors own all copyrights not held by the publisher.

The information herein is offered for informational purposes solely and is universal as so. The presentation of the information is without a contract or any type of guarantee assurance.

The trademarks that are used are without any consent, and the publication of the trademark is without permission or backing by the trademark owner. All trademarks and brands within this book are for clarifying purposes only and are the owned by the owners themselves, not affiliated with this document.

Table of Contents

Introduction 1

Chapter 1: An Introduction to Reiki 3

    Reiki Healing to Restore the Balance of Internal Energy 4

    What Can I Expect from a Reiki Healing Session? 6

    The Science of Reiki 7

    A Brief History of Reiki 8

Chapter 2: Benefits of Reiki 11

    Increased Ability to Deal with Negative Energies and Stresses of the World 12

    Ability to Heal Others 13

    Physical Healing 14

    Mental and Emotional Healing 15

    Increased Spirituality 15

Greater Compassion 16

Stress Relief 17

Detoxifies the Body and Mind 18

Energizing and Rejuvenating 18

Step 1: Connecting with Reiki Energy 20

Step 2: Performing an Aura Scan 26

Step 3: Setting Your Intention 30

Step 4: Activating Reiki Symbols 32

Step 5: Guiding the Energy 35

Step 6: Closing the Connection 36

Healing Others Using Reiki 37

Chapter 4: General Advice for Maximizing the Results of Your Reiki Session 43

Setting the Environment 43

Mind-Body Alignment is Necessary 44

Understanding Your Chakras 45

Breathing in Reiki Energy............................63

Chapter 5: Advancing Your Reiki Practice.....65

　The Three Degrees of Reiki..........................65

　Reiki Attunement 67

Chapter 6: Additional Therapies to Use with Reiki 73

　Crystal Therapy 74

　Pray or Meditate..76

　Yoga 78

　Serve Others 79

　Nourish Your Soul...................................... 80

　Be Mindful in Your Experience 81

Conclusion...83

Introduction

Reiki healing has been around for thousands of years, though it has only recently piqued a worldwide interest. It is a practice that can be done by anyone with the proper training—and this book is going to provide that for you.

As you read, you will learn about the many benefits of Reiki and how it can heal you physically, emotionally and mentally. You will learn about the theory and the practice, as well as how to heal both yourself and others. As you advance, your ability to heal will become more pronounced and you can even learn to give Reiki to others across a distance.

Finally, this book will touch on some of the other techniques that may be used in addition with Reiki. This will heighten your spiritual connection to the world around you and help you connect to the healing energies of the world.

Happy reading!

Chapter 1: An Introduction to Reiki

Reiki (ray-kee) healing has Japanese origins. The meaning of Reiki is „Universal Life Force,' being made up of the terms „rei' (which translates to universal) and „ki' (which translates to life force). The goal of Reiki healing is generally to access the life force. Once it is flowing freely, it is directed in a way that heals the body.

The energy flow spoken of in Reiki healing comes from a universal force, which is believed to exist in all life forms. If you consider the difference between someone who is dead and living, the simplest way to explain it is that one contains energy, while the other does not. Our bodies are constantly at work, maintaining our breathing and other bodily functions, healing our injuries and sickness and keeping us alive—

even when we are sleeping. It is energy that allows this to happen.

Reiki Healing to Restore the Balance of Internal Energy

Many forms of Eastern medicine believe that illness comes from blocked energy channels. Reiki is intended to remove these blockages and help healing energy flow freely through the body. These blockages often result from a lifetime of experiences—negative emotion like anger, jealousy, fear, greed, and temptation can upset this balance. In addition to negative experiences, our channels may be blocked from not taking care of our physical bodies. Eating a diet that is low in nutritional value, not getting enough water, and being sedentary can also cause blockages in energy. Sometimes, our own minds can also get in the way of the positive energy field, as our doubts about ourselves and the doubts that others have of us cloud our judgment and our flow of healthy energy.

A good way to look at this restoration of energy is to imagine yourself as a hollowed-out pipe that has been left at the bottom of a riverbed. When you come into the world as an infant, you have not yet been harmed by the negative emotions and experiences in the world. Nobody has made you question your self-worth and there is no reason not to believe the world is a good place. As clean water continues to flow through this hollow pipe, things go well. The body is capable of great healing and maintaining a high state of health. Over time, however, the negative energies, thoughts, and general dirt of the world collect inside this pipe. As it sticks to the walls of the pipe, there is less energy flow. Over time, the flow of energy may stop altogether.

What Can I Expect from a Reiki Healing Session?

Many newbies to the world of Reiki energy and natural healing may choose to work with a professional for their first few sessions. It is important to remember that Reiki sessions only restore the natural flow of wholesome energy through your body. You may be aware of the sensations of energy as they fill you, but you typically notice the benefits after the session. You will notice the benefits in the way that you interact with the negativities of the world around you. You will also notice how the healing energy helps heal you from ailments and complaints, but this happens over time. Reiki stimulates the body's natural healing process. Though many people have Reiki experiences that they refer to as „miracles,' the reality is that the body and the energy flowing through it cause the healing—not the session itself. Often, it takes time for the effects to begin.

The Science of Reiki

The research on Reiki is fairly new, though this should not come as a surprise since Western medicine has only started to scratch the surface of more holistic, alternative treatments. While some studies have disputed the presence of this energy, it is believed that Reiki works because of the overall relaxation and healing environment that it provides to the body. By allowing the body to exist in a more relaxed, stress-free state, it encourages the body's natural healing processes. This can be seen in the many stories of miracles of Reiki and how it has healed people—whether their pain was physical, emotional, or mental. Reiki promotes all-over body wellness, unlike Western medicine, which relies on the treatment of symptoms rather than trying to heal the body and encourage long-term health and healing.

A Brief History of Reiki

The man credited for establishing the Reiki practice of modern medicine is Mikao Usui, a Sensei and Japanese monk. He was the first to publish literature on the topic and establish a basic framework for Reiki practice. Even though this was the first time that Reiki had been regulated, research shows that at least four types of Reiki had been practiced across Japan prior to Usui's work. With this framework came the passing down of knowledge through different generations of monks, healers, and scientists. It is common practice that for someone to practice Reiki, they must receive training from a teacher in the subject. Reiki teachers typically practice themselves and they pass down their knowledge and techniques to students.

According to stories, Usui searched for many years to find a way to heal himself and others through his hands, without having to tap into and deplete his own energy stores. He studied in China, studied Buddhism, and even took a 21-day course on a mountain that involved fasting, meditation and prayer. Usui's quest ended at the end of that 21-day course when he found Sanskrit symbols in the caves. It was not long before Usui would take this knowledge and set up a clinic, helping bring Reiki to the people around him, both teaching others and healing the world. These initial teachings focused heavily on how people could heal themselves, with the belief that people could not use their life energy to heal others unless they first healed themselves. It is recorded that Usui taught 16 different Reiki healers before his death and these healers would carry on his knowledge and teach a new generation of healers.

Modern-day Reiki in the United States was brought by Japanese-American Hawayo

Takata in 1937. Born in Hawaii, she spent an extended time in Japan completing Reiki training. When she returned to the United States, she would pass down her knowledge and techniques. Today, its use is widespread across different continents of the world, usually being labeled as a form of holistic or alternative medicine.

Chapter 2: Benefits of Reiki

One of the biggest questions you may have is, "Why Reiki?" There are dozens, possibly even hundreds, of forms of meditation, yoga and other holistic healing practices designed to promote this overall feeling of wellness and stave off sickness and negative emotions. Even though there are many options, Reiki sets itself apart because of how easy it is—you can do it anywhere, without any equipment, at any time of the day. Aside from the convenience factor, this chapter will go over some of the benefits of regular Reiki practice.

Increased Ability to Deal with Negative Energies and Stresses of the World

We cannot always control who we interact with. Even in the best careers, we might have to work with people that give off generally bad energies or who take advantage of others. You may pick up negativity from encountering an angry person at the bus stop or the coffee shop. You might even have your own negative emotions to deal with, as feeling saddened or angry at times is part of the human experience.

The benefit of Reiki is that it helps relieve of the weight of any negative experiences you may have. As you walk through your office building or down the street, you will notice a new recognition for those things that do not serve your purpose. You will understand what things do not serve your purpose in life and which encounters leave you in an undesirable mental state. Then, you can learn to block the energies from things you do not want to experience and avoid those situations that you can, should they not promote the satisfied, energized feeling that you should feel.

Ability to Heal Others

If you decide to progress past the point of Reiki healing for yourself, it is easy to become attuned with the world and direct your energy in a way that corrects the energy flow of others. As you choose people to practice with, it is important to choose those that are opened to the idea of Reiki healing. You may find yourself put off of the practice altogether if you try it on a relative with health problems who does not have an open mind to new age topics like Reiki. Keep in mind that it is not always your failure. Reiki will not work on someone who cannot open their mind and body to the flow of energy.

Physical Healing

Physical healing is one of the benefits of Reiki that people seem to be most skeptical about. They do not understand how something that restores energy can help relieve the symptoms of their physical condition, whether it is a simple headache or a chronic illness. Those who doubt this method have often been healed using a Western form of medicine, which commonly focuses on treating the ailment directly instead of using a full-body approach. This is one of the reasons that people turn to alternative or holistic medicine when a more scientific approach has healed them. In many cases, the results have been a complete turnaround. There are even anecdotes of people who have turned to Reiki healing and other alternative medicines and had success in healing cancer, relieving chronic pain, and fighting off severe illness.

Mental and Emotional Healing

People's pain and sickness are not always visible. Many people struggle with anxiety, depression, repressed emotions, and other mental and emotional states. They may not even be aware of their emotional state or what is causing it. Reiki does not always help you heal emotions unless you deal with them, however, it can make you more aware of your emotional state. This awareness can help you understand your problems. It can also help you tap into the divine nature and understand your purpose in life. As you continue to connect to the energy that exists within everything and all around you, it can help cultivate more positive emotions in your life, including connectedness, love, intimacy, kindness, compassion, and sharing.

Increased Spirituality

The flow of energy that you experience with

Reiki can help you notice the interconnectedness between all the life forms of earth. As you connect to all that is living around you, you will feel a greater connection to the divine. You will also feel as if you are part of something greater than what exists in your immediate world. For many people, this creates the feeling of being connected to something great and powerful. It offers reassurance that you are present in the Universe and you know that you are loved by and connected to the spiritual beings, both living and non-living that you may encounter through your day.

Greater Compassion

The connectedness that you feel when regularly cleansing and connecting to your internal source of energy can help you find greater compassion for all that exists in the world. You will be more compassionate and empathetic when you encounter others who are in pain, whether emotional or physical. You will also be more tolerant and understanding of others, aware that you cannot possibly understand their specific situation. As you learn this deep compassion for others, you will also learn to be kinder to and have greater compassion for yourself. This can help heal people who struggle with emotional trauma or low self-esteem, as they often struggle with treating themselves as well as they would treat others.

Stress Relief

Stress relief is a major benefit of Reiki, as it is responsible for many of its effects. When you regularly relax and provide yourself with stress relief, it gives your body and mind a much needed break from the fast-paced world around you. This stress relief can help you sleep better at night and promotes a stronger immune system since your body is getting the support that it needs to be healthy. This can also reduce blood pressure.

Detoxifies the Body and Mind

A major part of the Reiki process is the removal of negative energies and toxins from your body. It cleanses the body and helps you naturally eliminate toxins that may have built up in your organs, digestive system, and bloodstream. You naturally encounter these toxins through your day—they are in some of the foods that you eat and the air that you breathe. Reiki also detoxifies the mind, clearing it of blockages that are stopping you from dealing with emotional trauma. This clearer state of mind and deeper understanding help you on the path to healing.

Energizing and Rejuvenating

Reiki is a very energizing practice. As you tap into your own spiritual energy and the connectedness between you and all that is in the Universe, you will feel your own energy grow.

You will feel reinvigorated as the life force flows through your body. Some Reiki experts also say that the rejuvenation from Reiki has the ability to postpone the aging process and promote overall vitality.

Reiki is something that can take several attempts to get right. By knowing the benefits, you can be sure you are committing to a healing process. Reiki is worth learning, whether you use it to improve the quality of your own life or learn to transfer your energy to heal someone else.

Chapter 3: How to Do Reiki on Yourself

Most people begin their journey of Reiki healing by practicing on themselves. It is necessary to start with yourself before healing others, as you must be physically and emotionally healed to be able to accept the healing energy of Reiki and channel it through your body. Though many people choose to take courses to ensure they are connecting to Reiki energy and using it to its full pot3ntial, it is possible to learn Reiki for beginners on your own. If you find yourself struggling, don't be afraid to look up tutorials or signup for a class nearby. This can help you take your Reiki connection and education to the next level.

Step 1: Connecting with Reiki Energy

Creating with Reiki energy is about connecting with a heightened state of consciousness. In this state, you are aware of your connection to the life energy that flows through all the Universe. It should flow through effortlessly. Though connecting with Reiki energy is only the first step of practicing Reiki, it can be the most challenging for beginners. Do not become discouraged if you struggle with connecting to this heightened state, especially if you have not practiced any type of meditation before.

There are two parts to connecting to the Universal energy. First, you must speak to the Universe, let go of your ego, and open the connection to the wisdom and energy of the Universe. Once you are an open conduit for energy, you may use a visualization technique to feel the energy flowing through you.

Reiki Invocation

When you enter the state of mind that allows you to connect to Reiki energy, you are connecting with the consciousness of Universal Energy. To do Reiki Invocation, it is as easy as speaking to this energy of the Universe and asking it for permission to conduct its energy as a healing channel. When you speak to the energy, you should have a calm and clear mind. Beginners sometimes start their session with a few minutes of meditation to get them in the right frame of mind. Once you are relaxed, you will be able to speak to the Universal consciousness aloud or silently.

It does not necessarily matter how you ask to connect to this Universal Energy. You should choose to speak with the energy in a way that aligns with your own beliefs. However, the overall goal should be to pass on a pure form of healing and unconditional love. Once you have decided what to say and are ready to speak to the universe, place your palms together and position your hands in front of your heart chakra, as if in prayer. This is done using the heart chakra because healing must come from a place of love. The heart is the core of the emotions and the core of the soul. Once you are ready, you might say something like:

"I call upon the energy of the Universe and the energy of all the Reiki conduits of the past, present, and future to take part in this healing session. I call these energies near to me to create a stronger connection to the Universal energy.

I ask that these energies give me the infinite wisdom to channel this energy. I ask that the power of the Universal Energy flows through me and allows me to conduct unconditional love and pure healing, as well as grants me the knowledge to use and direct this energy where it is needed most.

I ask to be empowered through the blessings and divine love of the Universe."

It is important as you ask for this permission that you allow your shift to focus. You should not be focusing on yourself or your own ego being granted the ability to heal. Instead, you must raise your own consciousness and allow your questions to raise your vibrational energy. You must be in line with the Universal Energy so that the energy can flow through you as if you are a channel for its healing benefits.

Notice how as you speak to the universe, you are asking permission to be a conduit. You are not asking to be a healer or to make your own decisions in healing but are instead asking to be a conductor for the knowledge and wisdom of the universe. For this to be effective, you must allow your ego to float away and align your beliefs with the Universal consciousness, which is a higher state of knowledge and truth.

As you settle into this greater power, you must let go of those beliefs that do not align with the laws of the Universe.

Visualizing Universal Energy Entering Your Palms

The Universal Energy is not something that you can physically see, as it exists beyond a physical level of reality. This is the reason you must allow your mind to enter an altered state of consciousness to connect to it. Visualization can help you „see" this connection beyond the realm of reality. As you bring that into your mind, you will physically feel the powerful energy of the Universe coursing through you. Here is an example of a visualization you may use:

Begin by closing your eyes and breathing in deeply. As you let go of this deep breath, see bluish-white energy beams as they surround you. These energy beams stretch from the ground, like threads connecting the grounds of the earth to the sky and beyond, connecting all that exists in the Universe.

As you become aware of these connections, feel yourself bathing in this light. Take another deep breath. As you release it, focus your energy on your palms, speaking to the Universal Energy around you. Breathe in the infinite light and call it into your palms, visualizing the light entering your body. As it flows through your body and out your palms, they glow with an energy that has a cool, white color. Now, you should be able to feel the Universal Energy radiating through your palms.

As you do the visualization technique, keep in mind that it does not matter what the energy looks like. While visualizing it can help, you should sense or feel how the energy appears. Not everyone can physically see this energy, but that does not matter. It is your willpower and your willingness to connect to the Universal energy. It is your thoughts and willpower, as well as your willingness to be used as a conduit for the energy of the Universe, which creates the reality of your ability to heal.

Step 2: Performing an Aura Scan

The way that people perceive the existence of auras is often incorrect. Your body does not create an aura or give off a type of visible energy. Rather, the aura describes a Universal energy. This energy surrounds all living things, but it is not really around it. A person's aura is not projected, as it exists within the body, too. The body is overlaid on the spiritual energy that is an aura.

Your aura is part of your energy system. It absorbs and puts off information, working much like the brain in the way that it is able to transmit and receive signals from the world. Everything that is inherently you exists within the aura, affecting its overall health. It is a collection of your vibration, as well as your memories, experiences, thoughts, and emotions. When you are experiencing a negative emotion, it can distort your aura and affect its health. For example, some negative thoughts may show up on your aura as a muddy, dark blob. Once it takes hold, this may present as a physical symptom.

Many people are aware that auras have different colors that transmit information about the mind and body. In addition to different colors, auras have properties including size, pattern, shape, and texture. The color also does not have to be solid, such as the case of certain textures or discolorations.

Doing an Aura Scan on Yourself

Once you have connected with the Universal energy, you should feel the energy around you. Close your eyes to help with your visualization of this energy. Then, position your hands so they are just above your head, with your palms facing your body. You should either use your dominant hand or both of your hands for this exercise. Hold your hand(s) out in front of you, anywhere from 2-10" away from your body.

Starting above your head, you are going to move your hands down your body. If you would like, you can stop at the different energy points (chakras) along the body. Often, you can help yourself understand the specifics of imbalances or blemishes in your aura by paying attention to the different chakras of the body and what each area relates to. You'll learn more about the specifics of each chakra in the next chapter.

The first time that you move your hands down your body do a quick overall pass from your head to your hips. The base of the spine holds the root chakra, which is the lowest. Notice how you feel overall to gauge your energy. Then, do a second pass and be aware of the differences you might feel in different areas. Some areas may feel as if the energy is thicker or thinner, either speeding your hand along or slowing it down as you pass through. You may also sense subtle vibrations or temperature differences. If an area feels cooler, it means that the energy is flowing out. If it feels hotter, more energy is being drawn inward.

When you do notices differences, it is because your energy may need assistance or because it is in a state of change. This is when you move onto the next step using a targeted approach. You will have more success with aura scanning the more you practice. As you have more Reiki sessions, you will also find that you are more in tune with your body and what it needs for your energy to flow freely.

Step 3: Setting Your Intention

Setting your intention is as simple as stating what you want. By knowing what blockages or disruptions you are experiencing, you can trace this back to the root problem. By using a targeted approach and directing Reiki energy, you can heal specific ailments. Some examples of problems commonly healed during a Reiki session include:

- Achieving Spiritual Balance
- Reduction of Pain
- Reduced Stress
- Promote Healing of Trauma
- Promote Healing of Obesity
- Restoration of Relationships

- Improved Sleep
- Connect to a Higher Purpose
- Ability to Overcome Addiction
- Increased Positivity in Emotional State

You can think of your intention as a message. You are communicating to the aura, whether your own or another person's. This communication states your desired outcome and by directing your energy to that outcome, it strengthens the results. For your message to be heard, it must be clear and strong. As the Universe grants this request, the aura reflects that intention and heals the body and/or mind.

Setting your intention can be greatly improved by using Reiki techniques in combination with visualization. As you are focusing on your intention, visualize the outcome. Visualize how the outcome will change your life. Feel yourself becoming happier and focusing on more positive things, like going out dancing with your friends or having more time to spend with your significant other. Focus on the pain going away or on resolving whatever is holding you back.

For visualization to work, it must be incredibly vivid. Imagine how you would feel if your intention were to come true. Feel the relief of pain, whether emotional or physical. Imagine how you would look and feel if you were able to overcome your weight loss struggles or how refreshed and invigorated you would feel if you were able to get a full night of sleep. If you are healing someone else, visualize the changes that may come about and how they would feel if you were able to heal them. Combining visualization with setting your intention can have profound benefits and increase your Reiki healing power.

Step 4: Activating Reiki Symbols

Reiki symbols are symbols that you create with your hands that improve your ability to heal, transmit energy, and more. There are several symbols commonly used during Reiki, depending on your intended purpose and whether you are practicing on yourself or someone else.

To learn how to tap into Reiki power on a deeper level, it can be helpful to learn these symbols. While they will be described here, it would be impossible to describe how to do them in writing. You can find tutorials, charts, and other guides online that will help you with activating Reiki symbols the proper way. You could also take a class or speak with a Reiki teacher about learning these symbols. The most commonly used Reiki symbols include:

- Cho Ku Rei (Power Symbol)- The power symbol can amplify many things. It is commonly used at the beginning of a Reiki session to help amplify healing energy, as well as provide spiritual protection that people need when they are connecting to the aura of others to heal them. It may also be used to empower other symbols or infuse food with energy.

- Hon Sha Ze Sho Nen (Distance Symbol) - This symbol is about enlightenment, peace, and unification. As it unifies, healers typically use it when they are healing someone across a distance. It can also be used to send attunements across distances, allowing people to open their chakras and be receptive to the wholesome, healing energy of the Universe.

- Sei He Ki (Mental & Emotional Reiki Symbol) - This symbol is ideal when you are trying to heal yourself (or someone else) mentally or emotionally. It is attuned to the energies of love and wellbeing in the universe. Not only does it create a calmer mental state, but it may also be used to help someone release negative energies or remove addictions.

- Dai KO Myo (Master Symbol) - As the name suggests, the Master Symbol is the most powerful in Reiki. Often, it is only Reiki Masters that can connect with this symbol. It is used to create wondrous life changes, to heal the soul, and to relieve the body of disease and illness in the aura.

Step 5: Guiding the Energy

One of the biggest mistakes that beginners in the world of Reiki healing make is believing that hand positions take priority over the other parts of the Reiki healing process. Things like being able to connect to the higher consciousness that allows you to access the energy of the Universe and setting your intention are much more important. However, it is possible to guide Reiki energy, especially when you are targeting a specific area of the body.

To direct Reiki energy, simply place your hands over the area you want to heal. Visualize and feel the energy flowing as you state your intention. If you are doing a full body Reiki session, then simply moving your hands over the body will be enough. As you guide the healing energy to the areas of your body that need it most, it is important to state your intention for each individual area you are trying to heal. Repeat steps 3-5 as many times as you need to before closing the connection. You will be finished when you can do an aura scan without feeling blockages or disruptions in energy.

Step 6: Closing the Connection

Another mistake that Reiki beginners often make is failing to close the connection between themselves and the Universe, or themselves and whoever they are trying to heal. When you fail to close the connection, you may absorb any negative energy that was released from your aura or the aura of the person you are trying to heal. If you do not close the connection, you can carry these emotions around and it may make you feel ill or exhausted.

The key to closing the connection is releasing any of the negative energies that have accumulated in your system. You can do this easily by visualizing all the negative energy flowing out of your body through your palms, releasing any negative energy that is stored in your system and leaving you in a rejuvenated state. As you connect with your typical energy, you will find yourself returning to your normal state of consciousness. Many people also wash their hands with cool water following a session to help them remove residual energies that may linger behind on the hands.

Healing Others Using Reiki

Doing Reiki on others is a new way to conduct your healing energy. While there are slight differences from performing the healing ritual on yourself, you will notice some similarities in the actual healing process.

Doing an Aura Scan on Someone Else

To do an aura scan on somebody else, you should begin by asking them to lie down. This will give you the best opportunity to sense their flow of energy through the different chakras. After you have opened your mind and body to the Universal Energy, visualize a white light that covers your body from head to toe. This white light will act as your shield, protecting you from absorbing any negative or unhealthy energy from the other person.

Use your dominant hand or both hands, as you would while sensing your own auras. Begin on the right side of the person's body and run your hands along the side, moving gradually but pausing for a few seconds at each chakra position (you can learn these positions in the next chapter). You will not need to hold your hands there as long after you get more practice. Make a mental note whenever you sense a disruption of the other person's aura. You will target this area later. If you cannot remember the area, keep a notebook and hand nearby and jot each area down. Then, do this with the left side of the body and make a mental note of any disruptions.

Now that you have done the initial scan place your hands over their body on problem areas, one at a time. Close your eyes as you place your hands over the block or negative energy and allow yourself to visualize the color, shape, size, and texture associated with the block. As you visualize the blocks, you should feel yourself becoming familiar with what is causing the blocks. These details can point to someone's unhealthy behaviors, recurring mental patterns, and unresolved emotions. Before a person will be able to clear their head and allow life energy to flow through their body, it is critical that they review and solve these issues.

Something to keep in mind is that you should not have to strain yourself to hear these messages. If you cannot understand the meaning behind someone's block, do not worry. You will come to understand more and connect to the Universal consciousness in a deeper way as you continue to practice.

Doing an Aura Scan across Distance

Some Reiki masters can heal across a distance, not only without physically touching someone but without the person being physically present. This healing is powerful and resonates through all the energy that makes up the world, forming a connection between the healer and the person they are trying to heal.

To begin healing across a distance, create a drawing on a sheet of paper. This should be a rough sketch of a body, though it does not have to resemble the person you are trying to scan. It is merely meant as a representation and reference sheet. Connect to Reiki energy as you would normally and visualize the white shield of light forming around you, protecting you from negative energies you may pick up while scanning your auras.

Begin by scanning using either your dominant hand or both hands. Scan the right side first, followed by the left, front, and back. You will do this by positioning your palm over different points on the sketch. If the connection is strong enough, you will experience a sensation of which areas of the body are blocked, much like you would if the person was lying in front of you. You should take note of these blocks and any messages that result. Then, you will use a blockage removal technique as you did before.

Following Up
After the initial scan when you are working with someone else, you should talk to them about

blockages or disruptions in their energy and what they could possibly mean. If you have received any messages from reading their aura, you should discuss them and point them out. While you may be able to heal someone's energy temporarily, the same blocks will resurface eventually unless the underlying problem is dealt with. Reiki can help with this, but other healing work may be necessary for total healing as well.

Healing

Once you have followed up after the aura scan, you are ready to heal. You can conduct the healing the same way you would with yourself. You must set your intention, activate the Reiki symbols, and guide the energy. Finally, you will want to close the connection. This is even more important when healing others than when healing yourself since you will leave yourself open to the negativities you have just dispelled from their aura.

Chapter 4: General Advice for Maximizing the Results of Your Reiki Session

The degree of healing that you experience after a Reiki session depends on several factors. The intensity of the session, your level of focus, and how open you are to the healing energy created during the session can all impact your effects. This chapter will provide some additional tips that can maximize the results of your Reiki healing session.

Setting the Environment

One of the great things about Reiki is that it doesn't need any extra equipment or space, so you can practice it anywhere. While you should practice Reiki somewhere you can focus, it does not need to be absolutely silent for you to connect to the healing energies of the Universe.

You may want to practice Reiki in your office building, for example, even as people hustle and bustle around you. As long as you can enter the right state of consciousness to connect to Reiki energy, you should not have any troubles. The goal is to choose an area where you can heal without resistance from your environment.

Many people also begin their Reiki session by washing their hands with cold water. Water is cleansing. It removes residual energy and purifies your immediate area. This will allow the healing energy of the Universe to flow freely from your hands, in its purest, most wholesome form.

Mind-Body Alignment is Necessary

There is no practice that cannot make you do what you do not want to do. People who resist the idea of energy flow or who do not believe in the authenticity of new age topics will have trouble experiencing the results of a Reiki session. You must be open and receptive to the idea of Reiki alignment and be aware of the energy as it flows through you. Once you have opened your mind and are receptive to the energies, you will become aware of the way that energy feels as it courses through your body. It is then, and only then that you will be able to experience the benefits.

Understanding Your Chakras

The chakras describe key energy points through the body. They have been studied for thousands of years, with the ancient texts called the Vedas detailing their abilities. The word „chakra" translates to „wheel" in Sanskrit, which makes sense as the chakras are considered the wheels of energy within the body. When the chakras are functioning well, they contribute to our existence and promote overall happiness and wellness in our lives. The chakra system is all about trying to achieve balance. When one chakra is under-active, or not active enough, other chakras may overcompensate. Each of the chakras governs a certain area or systems of the body. By understanding which areas of the body are affected by the chakras and paying attention to the messages received through aura scans, you can properly balance each area. This allows you to perform Reiki where it is needed most.

Muladhara (Root Chakra)

The first of the chakras is the root chakra, which is sometimes considered the „seat" of the soul since all the chakras sit upon this chakra and it channels the body's connection to the earth. The root chakra channels red light energy and it is located near your tailbone, between the base of your spine and belly button. It is common for the root chakra to become overactive since it is heavily used. When it is balanced, the root chakra makes you feel grounded. You should feel deeply rooted in your human experience. You should also feel a sense of peace and accomplishment when you think about your life in terms of safety, shelter, and money.

The root chakra affects your day-to-day life. For most people, the balance feels like financial and emotional security. When the root chakra is overactive, it can cause jitteriness and anxiety. This comes from a place of worry and fear, generally regarding one's survival. Anxiety problems can cause more than just jitteriness- it may cause lower back issues, digestive problems, hip pain, prostate problems in men, and ovarian cysts in women. An over-active root chakra may make you feel nervous, fearful, or unwelcome in your environment. When this chakra is over-active, it can also cause people to act greedy and materialistic. They may resist change and be obsessed with their overall sense of security. When the root chakra is under-active, which can happen when people have not struggled with their sense of security to life, it may cause them to be distant or „spaced out.' People may describe them as not having their heads in the clouds.

You can encourage the balancing of this chakra by taking care of your survival needs. Otherwise, after being balanced, the chakra will act up again. However, you will find yourself with enough energy to do this after recharging the chakra. When you need to create calm in yourself, use the root chakra to focus on your connection to your spirit. People often care for this chakra by spending time in nature, connecting to spirit guides, meditating, or praying. Acts of compassion and volunteering can also help, as kindness helps guide overactive energy away from the root chakra and power the other centers of the body.

Svadhishana (Sacral Chakra)

The second chakra translates to „the place of thy self.' The sacral chakra is the home of your creative energy. It is located just above the root chakra and just below the belly button, and the sacral chakra's orange, glowing power is connected to the human experience. The sacral chakra is also about pleasure, so when it is balanced, you will be able to enjoy the pleasures of life without overdoing them. This includes eating good food, having sex, and enjoying creative activities. These will nourish you and provide a sense of wellness and abundance.

If the second chakra is overactive, it can cause people to overindulge. This can cause problems like gluttony and addiction. A good sign that the chakra is over-stimulated is guilt that comes along with your pleasurable activities. You should not have to feel guilty about pleasure. Another cue of an imbalanced chakra system is trouble enjoying things that should be nourishing, like nutrient-dense, flavorful foods or sex with someone that you care about. Physically, problems with this chakra can cause hormone imbalances, addiction, restlessness, and obesity.

Ideally, you should balance the second chakra by consciously drawing the energy given to the pleasure center into the heart. It is easy to balance the sacral chakra, simply by asking yourself each time that you do something, "Is this activity good for me? Is it nourishing and healthy? What benefits could come from this activity?" As you assess your actions, you are taking the steps necessary to recognize those activities that do not suit your heightened consciousness and healthy existence. This gives you the insight needed to know when you need to draw energy from the sacral chakra and move it into the heart.

You may also need to balance this chakra by allowing energy to flow through it. When your sacral chakra is underactive, it may be indicative of you practicing things and working without having the time to enjoy yourself. This can cause problems like decreased sex drive, impotence, depression, and a lack of creativity and passion. When the chakra is underactive, you can energize it by making an effort to enjoy life. It can be hard to find time for pleasure when you lead a busy life, but it is important to do so if you want to avoid chakra imbalance.

Manipura (Solar Plexus Chakra)

The Sanskrit for the third chakra translates to „lustrous gem.' This is considered the gem of the soul, as it is where you create a sense of identity, self-confidence, and personal power. The solar plexus can be found just below the ribs, above the belly button and below the center of your chest. When it is balanced, you will have insight into life's situations and the wisdom to know when a situation is not right for you. You will also feel a sense of personal power in your life's situations, knowing that you are in control rather than feeling as if you are only along for the ride. The yellow energy from this chakra glows bright and is often called the warrior chakra, as it gives you the confidence to excel and the wisdom to be familiar enough with your personal truth that you know what you are fighting for.

When the solar plexus chakra is out of overactive, it becomes apparent in the way that the power we have over our own lives begins to spill over into the lives of other people. This creates a desire to micromanage others and exercise total control. It can also make you greedy, quick to anger, and lacking in empathy and compassion. Physically, this can cause digestive issues and imbalances of the internal organs, including the kidney, liver, pancreas, and appendix. To bring about balance, you can open your heart and focus on compassion and love. Meditate and focus your intention on projecting love and kindness the people around you. Rather than allowing your chakra to focus on your own needs, visualize yourself as a beacon of love.

The solar plexus may become blocked when our ability to control our own life's circumstances are taken away. This can make you feel indecisive, needy, timid, and insecure. To reconnect and reenergize the third chakra, spend time reflecting on your abilities and talents. Everyone has something they are good at. Now, make a list of all the things you would say you are „good" at. You do not have to be especially talented at them—it's okay if you are an artist, but not Picasso. Empower yourself by creating affirmations and reflecting on those things that give you empowerment and make you the person you are.

Anahata (Heart Chakra)
The Sanskrit for Anahata translates to „unhurt.' The heart chakra is associated with green

energy and it is known as the center of love, empathy, kindness, and compassion. This includes not only the love you hold for others but the love you have for yourself. It is located near the center of your chest, between the throat and breastbone.

When the heart chakra is balanced, you will find yourself feeling love equally for yourself and others. This allows you to meet your commitments while leaving yourself time for the self-care you need. Additionally, when you or someone else goes through troubles, you can still see the kindness and compassion that radiates from within them.

When the heart chakra is overactive, it can cause you to make unhealthy choices. You forget personal boundaries and are driven by your desire to love. Often, this presents as finding yourself putting the needs of others before yourself. However, it is important to remember that you cannot pour from an empty cup and you must also find time to love yourself. Treat yourself with the same level of kindness, forgiveness, and compassion that you would treat others. Physically, an overactive heart chakra can cause intense heartburn, problems with interpersonal relationships, heart palpitations, and a fast heart rate. The key to balancing your heart chakra is finding the time that you need for yourself. Commit to doing something for yourself at least once per day. You could do a self-massage (or have someone do it for you), take a relaxing bath, or do something that you truly enjoy. As you set your intention and meditate, you should focus on sending yourself the compassion that you give so selflessly to others.

If the heart chakra is underactive, it can cause problems of the heart. This sometimes happens as a result of heartbreak and other harsh lessons of the world. When you cannot stop yourself from taking these lessons of life personally, it can cause your heart chakra to be blocked. This could be compared to building a wall around your heart, causing you to struggle to get close to others and to share pieces of yourself. This presents physically as circulation problems and the feeling that you are not present in your body. You may go through life on autopilot, simply living your life without any emotional attachment. As most people work hard to build the defenses around their heart, it can be hard to knock them down as well. You should start with self-care to energize your heart chakra. As you find yourself able to project love and compassion on yourself, begin to project on the world around you again.

Vishuddha (Throat Chakra)

Vishuddha translates to „very pure" which relates to the chakra's ability to reveal and connect to your personal traits. It is the center of communication and allows you to speak your truth with clarity. It is located right above the heart and has a bright blue energy. When you are balanced, you find yourself with the knowledge to decide which words are appropriate for the situation. While you will speak clearly with truth, love, and kindness, you will also have the enlightenment to speak out against things that are unkind or unjust. Having a balanced throat chakra can also create inspiration and enlightenment for those around you.

The fifth chakra often becomes overactive when we struggle with having our voice heard for some reason, usually accompanied by feelings of being invalidated or ignored. As you do not feel like you are being heard, the throat chakra can cause you to interrupt others, speak loudly, or simply talk a lot. Physically, people who struggle with an overactive throat chakra may suffer from mouth ulcers, cavities, frequent infections, and throat pain. To bring about balance to an overactive throat chakra, you must get in the habit of thinking before you speak. Instead of blurting the first thing that comes to mind, ask if what you are saying is true, necessary, and kind. If so, then you should continue to speak.

Over time, failing to speak your personal truth can cause you to shut down. People may refer to you as quiet or shy and you may find yourself unable to express what you are feeling to others, even in times of crisis or upset. It is not uncommon for digestive issues to result from an underactive throat chakra, since the emotions may be swallowed down instead of being set free. The best way to start energizing this throat chakra is to practice speaking about your feelings and your personal truths. Even allowing your own ear to receive these truths can help give your chakra the energy it needs.

Anja (Third Eye Chakra)
This chakra, translating to "beyond wisdom," opens your mind in a way that you can perceive

the world beyond your five natural senses. For some people, this presents only as an intuition. For others, a balanced third eye chakra can result in psychic energy or extrasensory perception. The third eye chakra is associated with the color deep purple or indigo and is located between the eyes, deep inside the forehead. The pineal gland of the brain is said to represent the third eye chakra. This is a small, pinecone-shaped gland that regulates your sleep and wake schedule.

The third eye chakra is balanced when you feel equally in tune with the spiritual and physical world. While you will receive information from something outside of your normal five senses, this emotion should not be presented in a way that overwhelms you. The third eye is heavily celebrated in many cultures, with the Ancient Egyptians, Indians, and other cultures recognizing its properties long before technology allowed brain scans to detect the pineal gland.

Aside from people who are heavily attracted to paranormal experiences, astrology, tarot card readings, and the like, it is difficult for the third eye to be over stimulated. Most people experience the opposite, as fluoride that is commonly found in water and other sources tends to accumulate on the pineal gland and affect third eye abilities. However, when people do experience an overactive third eye, as well as those who have psychic powers, may be overwhelmed by their insight from the world. It can become distracting and take away from the physical human experience. If you do find yourself distracted from the human experience, take some time being a human. Go to the beach and immerse your toes in the sand or stick your feet in a stream in the woods. Immerse yourself in the experience, stating, "I am a human being. I am a human doing".

The world that we live in typically invalidates the development of intuition and psychic abilities, as those things that cannot be physically seen or proven with science are often said not to exist. For this reason, people are more likely to have an underactive third eye chakra than an overactive one. When your third eye chakra is underactive, it can cause you to disconnect from spiritual experiences. Some common problems that result include allergies, sinus troubles, and headaches. Meditation is the best way to energize the sixth chakra. First focus on the signals outside your body, then spend time listening to your spirit and realizing its place in the world. As you continue to practice, connecting with the third eye will become easier.

Sahaswara (Crown Chakra)
The final chakra is the seventh chakra, which is located just above the head. It has an energy unlike any of the other chakras, as it connects us to the entire Universe. One way to think of it is

a seed of conscious energy that rests above your head, encouraging your connection to all that is around you. The crown chakra is associated with a violet and white energy. When it is balanced, you may feel as if you are a spiritual warrior. While most people do not reach the state of perfect balance in their lifetime, as it is similar to the Buddhist concept of Nirvana. It is the overcoming of suffering and death when the soul has achieved its highest state of ascension. However, it is not necessarily achieving this that creates balance with the crown chakra, as most people take several lifetimes or longer to conquer their ascension. It is the journey of achieving this balance and moving upward. It is the journey and the progression that brings wisdom, good health, and happiness.

It is not possible for the crown chakra to be overactive, as it is connected to the energy of the Universe. It is impossible to exist in the physical world and be overcome with energy from consciousness, so it is not important to balance. However, the crown chakra is commonly underactive. Most people have an underactive crown chakra, as it feels exactly like a human experience. You can raise the energies of your seventh chakra by balancing your other chakras and practicing spiritual development. Doing things like meditating and connecting with the consciousness will invigorate your crown chakra. Be sure to focus on all the chakras and not just the crown chakra, as the crown chakra cannot be stimulated unless all the other chakras are in balance.

Breathing in Reiki Energy

One technique that you can use to amplify your Reiki energy is to breathe it and imagine the life force filling you. Close your eyes and deeply breathe through your nose, deep enough that if there were someone sitting next to you, they would audibly hear your breath sounds. As you inhale, feel the energy of life filling you with breath. Feel the energy as your chest and stomach expand, filling you up with breath.

Now, as you exhale, feel your body becoming soft. As the breath leaves you, everything relaxes. If you have trouble connecting to Reiki energy, preparing in this way lets you connect to Reiki energy and feel the life force. It is most useful before you use visualization to imagine the force of the Universe flowing inside of you.

Chapter 5: Advancing Your Reiki Practice

You should always begin your Reiki practice by doing sessions on yourself. Once you are confident in healing yourself, if you have the desire to, you can also learn to heal the flow of energies through other people. It is generally advised once you are ready to advance your practice that you learn from a professional. However, this chapter will guide you through the basics.

The Three Degrees of Reiki

Reiki practice is something that has different levels, with the lowest level being reserved for people who want to practice Reiki on themselves and the highest level being reserved for people who learn from and become Reiki masters.

First Degree Reiki

First Degree Reiki is the main focus of this book. This involves self-care and is training that allows you to practice Reiki in daily life. Many people trained in First Degree Reiki can also place their hands on family and friends to promote Reiki healing. It is not uncommon for people in the healthcare field to learn First Degree Reiki, as it can be used as a complementary medicine. Usually, massage therapists, nurses, and other people who are in a profession where it is appropriate to touch patients will study First Degree Reiki.

Second Degree Reiki

Second Degree Reiki is practiced across a distance. It is ideal for situations where touch might not be possible or when it is inappropriate, such as in the case of psychotherapists who may want to learn Reiki to help patients to process emotional trauma. Second Degree Reiki relies on creating a mental connection, rather than a hands-on approach. In other situations, the mental connection may be established to enhance the effects of the Reiki session and promote a greater flow of energy.

Third Degree Reiki

Third Degree Reiki is the highest level, being achieved only by Reiki masters. To officially earn certification as a Reiki master, it is generally accepted that you must receive an invitation from an existing Reiki master. The people who are extended this invitation are those who have devoted their lives to the practice of Reiki and teaching it to others. Since it requires an invitation from a Reiki master, Third Degree Reiki is generally learned through a long apprenticeship.

Reiki Attunement

A major component of practicing Reiki is the vibrational frequencies. You can only channel the healing energies of the Universe that you have been attuned to. It is not uncommon for a Reiki attunement to be performed before someone moves up to the next degree of Reiki since increasing your vibrational frequency will give you the opportunity to increase your healing potential.

A Reiki attunement can be done by a Reiki teacher who possesses the ability to open your chakras in a way that allows a higher state of consciousness to flow through you. To have the ability to make your energy flow through someone else, these chakras must be able to put forth and absorb energy, connecting you to the flow of life energy in the universe and allowing you to channel it through someone else's body. The process of Reiki attunement may also be called expanding your energy channels. If you do not want to work with a Reiki teacher, then you may also be able to raise your vibrational frequency by doing Chi exercises, which will be discussed next.

Alternatively, you can work on balancing and then energizing each of your chakras on your own. While this may take longer and require a greater deal of focus than when working with a Reiki master, it is a great alternative if you do not have access to a Reiki instructor. Below, you'll find guidelines for opening each of the chakras. As you read the chants, keep in mind that „A' is pronounced „ah' when chanting and „M' is pronounced like „mng,' as if it has an „ng' like the word thing.

- Crown Chakra- To open the crown chakra, place your hands in front of your stomach. Allow the ring fingers to point upward and touch at the tips before crossing the other fingers, ending with the left thumb being positioned under the right. Once your hands are in position, begin to focus on the crown chakra. You may visualize this as a white or purple light above the head if you would like. Then, chant the sound NG. As a note, you should not use this to open the crown chakra unless you have a solid foundation upon the root chakra.

- Third Eye Chakra- Sit somewhere you are comfortable and bring your hands to the lower part of your chest. Place your hands so the middle fingers are straightened, with each touching at the tip and pointing forward. Then, bend the other fingers so that they touch near the top at the second joint. Allow the thumbs to touch as well, pointing toward your body. Now, focus on the third eye where it is located above the eyebrows. As you visualize its indigo energy, chant the sound AUM.
- Throat Chakra- To open the throat chakra, position your hands so your fingers overlap each other on the inside. Allow the thumbs to touch near the top,

then pull them up slightly so they stick out. You may position your hands near your chest. Focus on the blue energy of the throat chakra, which is located at the base of the throat. While you do this, chant the sound associated with this chakra—HAM.

- Heart Chakra- You should begin opening the heart chakra by sitting in a cross-legged position. Bring your index finger and thumb together to form a circle. Then, place your right hand just above your solar plexus and place the left hand on the left knee. Focus on the green, glowing energy of the heart chakra, right near your chest. The sound associated with this chakra is YAM.
- Navel Chakra- To open the navel chakra, position your hands on the area just below your ribcage and above your stomach. Let your fingers join together,

palms against each other with the fingers pointing directly outward. Let the thumbs cross and be sure the fingers are straight. Now, focus on the area above the navel and see it as a ball of glowing yellow energy. As you visualize this energy and feel it course through you, chant the sound RAM.

- Sacral Chakra- You should open the sacral chakra while in a sitting position. Place your hands in your lap with the palms facing skyward. Let them overlap, with the left hand on the bottom and its palm touching the back of your fingers on your right hand. Once your hands are in position, allow the tips of the thumbs to come together. Now, focus on the energy in your lower back and navel, imagining it as a glowing orange ball of energy. When you are ready, begin chanting VAM.

- Root Chakra- Open the root chakra by bringing your thumb and index finger together at the tip, so they form a circle. Focus on the root chakra, imagining a glowing red ball of energy if you would like. As you feel the power of the root chakra, chant the sound LAM.

Before you settle into a chant to open one of your chakras, be sure that you are relaxed. It is best to fall into a meditative state of mind beforehand. This will give you the focus and attention that you need to bring about change with your chanting.

Chapter 6: Additional Therapies to Use with Reiki

Often, Reiki is not used as a standalone therapy. While it can produce results on its own, especially when it is performed by someone that has earned the title of Reiki Master, there are additional therapies that can be used to increase the results of Reiki healing. This chapter will go over some of them so that you can get the most of your Reiki healing sessions.

Crystal Therapy

Crystals are made up of elements of the earth. They carry a unique vibrational energy depending on what they are made out of. This vibrational energy allows them to attune to your body, producing certain effects. It is not uncommon for people to wear certain stones or carry them around. They can also be used during Reiki and other practices, as a way to enhance the results.

To add crystals to your Reiki session, you can put your hands into position over the chakras as you focus your intention and your healing energy. Hold the appropriate crystal in your hand and channel the energy into yourself or the person you are healing. The crystal that you use depends on which chakra you are trying to heal, excite, or calm. You can choose whichever crystal has the strongest pull or seems to call to you, or you can choose one that goes with the specific chakra you are trying to heal. Here are some of the crystals that should be used for each of the chakras:

- Crown Chakra- Clear Quartz, Diamond, Ametrine, Clear Calcite, Amethyst/Violet
- Third Eye Chakra- Lazuli, Lapis/Indigo, Quartz, Sodalite
- Throat Chakra- Turquoise/Blue, Celestite, Blue Lace Agate, Aquamarine
- Heart Chakra- Pink Calcite, Emerald/Green, Rose Quartz, Tourmaline
- Solar Plexus Chakra- Amber/Yellow, Malachite, Aragonite, Moonstone, Topaz
- Sacral Chakra- Carnelian, Orange

Stones, Smoky Quartz, Red Jasper
- Root Chakra- Lodestone/Red, Bloodstone, Tiger's Eye, Ruby, Garnet, Hematite

Something to keep in mind is that crystals can take on negative energy as people would. Some people choose to release negative energy on their crystal by performing a Reiki session to clean the crystal's aura before their own. There are several other options, including burning sage to cleanse the crystal or soaking it in saltwater. Some people also bury their crystals in salt, especially if they are soft and will be harmed by a saltwater bath. To amplify the power of a crystal, you can stick it on a windowsill or in direct moonlight. This works best when the moon is highly visible.

Pray or Meditate

Many people stay away from the prayer option because they believe they must claim a religion or choose a specific God if they are to pray. However, prayer does not have to be directed at anyone or anything specific. If you are not comfortable praying, you could also meditate.

This is a time when you should focus on your intentions. Get in the habit of focusing on the positives of what you want. Instead of saying that you do not want pain, say that you want to heal. Even when you say something negatively, by reflecting on it as you meditate, you are giving it your focus and energy. This can draw that thing into your life or cancel out what you are trying to achieve with the prayer.

You should always look at meditation and prayer as an opportunity to reflect and look inward. Even if you are speaking outward, whether to your God, the Universe, or whatever you believe in, it is important to look inward. Speaking out loud can help trigger insights that you may not have realized otherwise.

It does not matter how long you pray or when you pray. Simply set aside time each day, whether a few minutes or longer. Make it a habit. If you can, speak out loud as you pray and really focus on the things that you need to be happy in your life.

Yoga

Yoga originally comes from India, however, it has recently become popular around the world. It is used for physical activity but also encourages the development of a more spiritual mindset. The type of yoga that you participate in has a lot to do with the effects, as the positions and breathing patterns have the ability to invoke certain results.

As you do yoga, you should always use the breathing practice called „Pranayama.' This type of breathing is necessary for people who are trying to bring results to their yoga session. It allows you to connect with the Universe, while improving your physical and mental strength, increasing your memory power, and even extending your lifespan. You can take a class for yoga. Alternatively, look up positions or videos online. You'd be surprised how much information is available once you know where to look!

Serve Others

We may do the things that our family, friends, and co-workers ask us regularly. However, fewer people take time out of their busy weeks to help those who truly need it. The reality is that every person is fighting a battle that nobody else understands. For example, someone who is homeless is not necessarily lazy—they are the result of a collection of life circumstances that could just as easily happen to you or me.

As you start to explore the world and help the people that truly need it, you will find yourself better prepared to help others. You will find a newfound sense of satisfaction in yourself and the responsibilities of life, as you realize that you can be responsible for more than just your normal day-to-day routine. As a person that connects to the Universe, you have the knowledge and wisdom to help those around you. Additionally, helping those who are less fortunate gives you the opportunity to gain your own maturity, strength, and knowledge when it comes to fighting battles in your life.

Nourish Your Soul

Nourishing the soul is all about learning those things that make you happy and bring you peace—and then making an effort to do them. When you work long hours, or have a hectic family life, it is hard to find time for yourself. It is important to remember that you owe yourself this nourishment. It is necessary for you to take care of yourself if you want to connect to the Universal consciousness and connect with others.

In addition to nourishing yourself by committing time to yourself, it is essential that you take care of your physical body and mind.

Be sure that you get enough sleep each night. Practice relaxation techniques if you need to. You should also choose nutrient-dense foods, rather than those that are filled with empty calories. By nourishing your body and mind, you will find yourself in the best possible state to encourage mental, emotional, and spiritual healing and wellness too.

Be Mindful in Your Experience

People lead busy lives. As you rush from task to task, when do you make time to slow down? Think back to the last time that you had a meal. Were you rushing to get back to whatever task you were doing before or even checking your emails while you ate? What about your last trip to the store or to work? Did you look around you as you went and observe the sights, or were you on autopilot mode as you just tried to get from A to B?

It is easy to become so immersed with the physical experience that we forget to slow down and experience the world in all its beauty. Instead of going on autopilot, make an effort to notice the things you are doing. When you are washing dishes or sweeping the floor, pay attention to the way the muscles move in your arms, shoulders, and back. As you eat, pay attention to the different flavors and textures you are getting from the food. Immerse yourself in the experience of eating and chew slowly enough that you can take it all in. Whenever you are driving or walking, notice your surroundings. Instead of staring at the carpet when you are rushing to your office in the morning, make an effort to smile at your coworkers. It doesn't take any extra time to move the muscles in your face. By immersing yourself in your human experience, you will find yourself more connected to your spiritual one as well.

Conclusion

Reiki healing allows you to connect with the energies of the Universe and use it in a way that encourages the body to heal itself. It can be used to treat aches and pains, overcome allergies and headaches, and even heal chronic or painful diseases. The results depend heavily on your abilities and your mindset, as it is important to be receptive to the Reiki energies for them to result.

Often, the emotional and physical health problems that we struggle with stem from blocked energy channels in the body. Energy channels can be blocked after certain life circumstances or from being neglected. As you learn to encourage the flow of Universal energy through your body, you can promote overall health and wellness. You can stop at learning to heal yourself or you can continue our practice to strengthen your abilities and possibly heal others.

Hopefully, this book has been able to help provide the foundation for Reiki knowledge that you can build upon later. For the time being, however, you should know what you need to put your Reiki skills to work. The only thing left to do is practice! Your abilities will strengthen with time and as you become more aware of the way that the energies of the universe and your body affect you.

Best of luck!

References

https://www.holisticshop.co.uk/articles/guide-reiki-healing https://reiki-bangalore.com/all-aboutreiki.shtml

http://healthmantra.com/reiki/reiki_notes.shtml https://reiki-bangalore.com/why-reiki.shtml

https://www.livescience.com/40275reiki.html

https://www.reiki.org/faq/HistoryOfReiki.html

https://www.reiki-for-holistic-health.com/

https://www.chakra-anatomy.com/benefitsof-reiki.html

https://www.takingcharge.csh.umn.edu/can-ilearn-reiki-myself

https://www.reikiinfinitehealer.com/lifeforcee

nergy-optimization

http://www.threshold.ca/reiki/Using-ReikiTo-Scan-Yourself.html

https://reikirays.com/12467/how-to-do-anaura-scan-in-person-distance-scanning/

file:///C:/Users/saman/Downloads/ultimateguide-connecting-reiki-energy.pdf

https://blog.mindvalley.com/7-chakras/

https://www.eclecticenergies.com/chakras/open https://reikirays.com/16881/crystals-reiki-abasic-guide/

https://spiritualray.com/spiritual-growthexercises

https://www.powerofpositivity.com/7exercises-for-spiritual-strength/

Made in the USA
Columbia, SC
07 November 2019